ME TOO
BUT NEVER AGAIN
#PartTwo

THE HEALING
Journey

Hanna Olivas and Adriana Luna Carlos

Along with Other Inspiring Women Warriors

Table of Contents

INTRODUCTION 5

TRANSFORMING PAIN INTO STRENGTH
By Adriana Luna Carlos 9

FAITH OF A MUSTARD SEED
By Hanna Olivas 17

MILITARY SEXUAL TRAUMA
By Kyla Biedermann 24

THE GIRL BEHIND THE SMILE
By Lisa Brennan 32

YOU ARE WORTHY AND YOU CAN HEAL FROM
CHILDHOOD SEXUAL ABUSE
By Melanie Starr 41

STUCK AT FIVE YEARS OLD
By Monica Linson 52

JOIN THE MOVEMENT! #BAUW 56

INTRODUCTION

She Rises Studios was created and inspired by the mother-daughter duo Hanna Olivas and Adriana Luna Carlos. In the middle of 2020, when the world was at one of its most vulnerable times, we saw the need to embrace women globally by offering inspirational quotes, blogs, and articles. Then, in March of 2021, we launched our very own Women's Empowerment Podcast: **She Rises Studios Podcast**.

It is now one of the most sought out Women based podcasts both nationally and internationally. You can find us on your favorite podcast platforms, such as Spotify, Google Podcasts, Apple Podcasts, IHeartRadio, and much more! We didn't stop there. Establishing a safe space for women has become an even deeper need. Due to a global pandemic, women lost their businesses, employment, homes, finances, spouses, and more.

We decided to form the She Rises Studios Community Facebook Group. An environment strictly for women about women. Our focus in this group is to educate and celebrate women globally. To meet them exactly where they are on their journey.

It's a group of Ordinary Women Doing EXTRAordinary Things.

As we continued to grow our network, we saw a need to help shape the minds and influences of women struggling with insecurities, doubts, fears, etc. From this, we created a global movement known as:

Me Too, But Never Again #PartTwo - The Healing Journey

Me Too But Never Again #PartTwo: The Healing Journey is a collection of personal stories from female survivors who have endured the trauma and abuse of sexual assault. This powerful book, written by survivors for survivors, offers hope to those on their own journey to recovery and becoming warriors.

Each story in Me Too But Never Again #PartTwo is told in an intimate and personal way, providing readers with an emotional connection to the authors' experiences, struggles, and triumphs. From overcoming depression and anxiety to reclaiming power over their lives, each story is unique yet inspiring. Through these real-life stories of courage and resilience, readers will find strength in knowing that they are not alone in their struggles.

This book provides valuable information and guidance on how to build resiliency through self-care practices such as mindfulness meditation, journaling exercises etc. For those who have survived sexual assault or other forms of violence against women – or those looking for support while they work through this difficult time – Me Too But Never Again #PartTwo: The Healing Journey offers a safe space for recovery with inspiring stories that show it's possible to find hope after hardship.

She Rises Studios offers:

- She Rises Studios Publishing
- She Rises Studios Public Relations
- She Rises Studios Podcast
- She Rises Studios Magazine
- Becoming An Unstoppable Woman TV Show
- She Rises Studios Community
- She Rises Studios Academy

We won't stop encouraging women to be Unstoppable. This is just the beginning of our global movement.

She Rises, She Leads, She Lives...

With Love,
HANNA OLIVAS
ADRIANA LUNA CARLOS
SHE RISES STUDIOS
www.sherisesstudios.com

Adriana Luna Carlos

Founder and CEO of She Rises Studios & FENIX TV

https://www.linkedin.com/in/adriana-luna-carlos/
https://www.facebook.com/adrianalunacarlos
https://www.instagram.com/sherisesstudios/
https://www.sherisesstudios.com/
https://www.srslatina.com/
https://fenixtv.app/

Adriana Luna Carlos is an accomplished web and graphic designer, author, and mentor with a passion for helping women succeed in life and business. With over 10 years of experience in graphic and web arts, Adriana has built a reputation as an innovative leader and entrepreneur. In 2020, she co-founded She Rises Studios, a multi-digital media company and publishing house that has helped countless clients achieve their branding and marketing goals. In 2023, she co-created FENIX TV, an online streaming platform that showcases stories of people breaking barriers, shattering stereotypes, and triumphing against the odds.

As an advocate for women's success, Adriana challenges her clients and mentees to strive for nothing less than excellence. She has a deep understanding of the insecurities and challenges that women often face in the business world and provides the guidance and resources needed to overcome them. Her success as a business leader and entrepreneur has made her a sought-after mentor and speaker at events around the world.

Through her work, Adriana has demonstrated a commitment to creating opportunities for women to succeed in business and life. Her passion for innovation, leadership, and women's empowerment has made her a respected figure in the business community, and her impact will undoubtedly continue to inspire and empower women for years to come.

TRANSFORMING PAIN INTO STRENGTH

By Adriana Luna Carlos

I remember the feeling of utter fear, shakiness in my body, overwhelming anxiety coursing through me. It's sad to say that the scariest day of my life was not even a day that any sexual abuse occurred. It was the day that I decided to tell my family of all that had been happening to me in the home I lived in for 10 years. This saddens me so much because somehow this perpetrator happened to make me fear exposing the truth more than I would fear enduring another day of his abuse.

If anyone has ever been a victim of sexual abuse, of any kind, the question that we despise the most is "why did you wait so long to speak up?" I wish for those who ask those questions, that they could feel how much that question hurts us. To ask that question is to presume that you could understand the gravity of what we went through, or if you have gone through it, that you are choosing to ignore your own experiences. Although you may not know it, you may unintentionally make someone feel ashamed by asking that question.

The truth of the matter is that we do not grow up thinking that one day we will have to explain why someone would violate us. It is not something that you immediately know how to cope with and we all process things differently and at different rates of time. Therefore, it does not matter "when" we spoke up, but rather that we did at all. The shame should be placed on the predator, we should ask them, "why did you choose to affect someone else's life forever?" The sad part is even if we do ever get this answer, it will not make us feel any better.

What I am writing today will not be an account of all the abuse I endured, but rather how did I heal after it and even to this day. If you are wanting to learn more about my story then start at the beginning with book one, Me Too But Never Again. In that book I go into some of the details of the abuse and the trauma that occured. Today, you will learn my personal mindset and an account of how I have been actively working towards healing. Because let me tell you, it is not something that can 100% be healed from and definitely not quickly. It's been 10+ years since the abuse and I still struggle at times to understand the "why" and work on the "how". The "why" being, "why did they choose to hurt me?" and the "how" being, "how can I overcome this?"

The Types of Sexual Abuse

To try to understand the impact of sexual abuse, we first have to understand the different types of abuse. Sexual abuse can take many different forms, and it's important to recognize that not all forms of sexual abuse may be immediately apparent or recognized by society. Here are some examples:

1. Physical sexual abuse: This involves any unwanted touching, groping, or sexual contact. This can include rape, sexual assault, and molestation.

2. Non-physical sexual abuse: This can include things like verbal harassment, sexual comments, and exposing oneself to another person without their consent.

3. Emotional sexual abuse: This can include things like manipulating someone into sexual activity, threatening someone if they refuse sexual activity, and using sexual acts as a way to control or manipulate another person.

4. Sexual exploitation: This can include things like child sexual abuse, human trafficking for sexual purposes, and using someone's vulnerability or need for basic resources like food, shelter, or money to coerce them into sexual acts.

5. Coercion or pressure: This can include things like using pressure, manipulation, or threats to force someone to engage

in sexual activity. This can also include situations where someone is unable to give full consent, such as if they are intoxicated or under the influence of drugs.

6. Online sexual abuse: This can include things like sexting, revenge porn, and online grooming. It can also involve online harassment or abuse that is sexual in nature.

7. Sexual abuse within relationships: This can include things like marital rape, sexual coercion within a romantic relationship, and sexual abuse within a familial relationship.

Understanding the Impact of Sexual Abuse

Sexual abuse is a traumatic experience that can have a profound impact on an individual's mental, emotional, and physical well-being. I understand all too well the impact that it can have on a person's life. The trauma of sexual abuse can linger long after the abuse has ended, leaving you to cope with the aftermath. One of the most profound impacts of sexual abuse is the psychological trauma that it causes. For a long time I had thought I was "good", that I wasn't struggling with what happened and it took time for me to see that I had residual and internal trauma that I had not faced.

It wasn't until I got in a relationship for the first time that I truly recognized the severity of the trauma, even more so once I was married. I thought that I was healed and that I had peace. But there were times when my significant other would do a simple act of love by leaning in for a kiss, and I would immediately get nervous and pull away. This is a person that I love and trust, and yet I had fear, "why was this?" I thought. I was baffled by my own inability to recognize my instinct to flee. My mind knew I was not in imminent danger but my body couldn't recognize this. This is particularly difficult for a logical person such as myself to not immediately understand myself.

This sense of self doubt caused a ripple effect of pain and shame. I hadn't truly felt the shame till I was in a relationship because growing up I knew that what was happening to me was not my fault or my doing. Yet, oddly enough once I was in a relationship that is when the shame hit. I was embarrassed to admit to myself that I was "damaged". And that's the thing, we all experience these stages in different points of our healing journey.

The memories and feelings associated with the abuse can be overwhelming, leading to anxiety, depression, and PTSD. The impact of sexual abuse can also extend to physical health. Survivors may experience chronic pain, headaches, and digestive issues. Sexual dysfunction is also common among survivors, making it difficult to engage in healthy sexual relationships.

It's important to recognize that healing from sexual abuse is a process, and that every survivor's journey is different. With the help of therapy, support groups, and other resources, survivors can learn to cope with the effects of sexual abuse and find a path towards healing and recovery. Remember that the impact of sexual abuse is not a reflection of one's worth.

Beginning the Healing Journey

Healing looks different for everyone, and there's no one-size-fits-all approach. What works for one person may not work for another, and that's okay. You have to find what works best for you and your situation. It might take some trial and error to figure out what works best for you and that's totally normal. No matter which direction you go in, remember that healing is a journey and it will not be fixed overnight. Here are some steps that I have learned along the way and that have served me well:

Step One: Accepting The Reality of The Abuse

The first step in beginning your healing process is accepting what has happened to you as real. Denial may be an easy way out but it will only make things worse in the long run. Acknowledging what has happened allows us to accept that we are no longer powerless over our past experiences, but instead empowered by them.

Step Two: Coping Mechanisms & Self-Care Strategies

As we start accepting our past experiences, it's important to learn healthy coping mechanisms and self-care strategies that will help us manage our emotions in a more productive way. This includes finding healthy ways to cope with stress like yoga, meditation or journaling; setting boundaries and practicing assertiveness; learning to regulate emotions; developing self-compassion; and practicing forgiveness and acceptance of ourselves. Self-compassion is an essential part of healing from abuse because it helps us give ourselves grace for where we are on our journey while still encouraging us toward progress. We must recognize that although we have been through difficult times doesn't mean that we deserve any less than compassion for ourselves - in fact, quite the opposite!

Step Three: Setting Boundaries & Practicing Assertiveness

Learning how to set boundaries can be incredibly empowering because it allows us to take back control over how people interact with us which was often taken away during these experiences. Practicing assertiveness is a great skill which helps build confidence by allowing one to voice their opinions without fear of judgment or backlash from others. This is something that many survivors struggle with due to previous trauma or mistreatment they may have experienced in the past.

<u>Step Four: Practicing Self-Forgiveness & Self Acceptance</u>

Part of beginning your healing journey is not just forgiving yourself but also accepting yourself - flaws and all. We all make mistakes along the way but it's crucial that we are able to understand this doesn't define who we are but rather they just add additional layers of complexity which make up each individual person's unique story!

<u>Step Five: Building Resilience and Finding Meaning</u>

The healing journey of sexual abuse is not an easy feat, but it is possible. I have learned that resilience is not something that we are born with, but rather something that we can develop over time. Resilience is about learning to cope with adversity, to bounce back from setbacks, and to find the strength to keep moving forward.

For me, building resilience has meant taking small steps towards healing every day. It has meant learning to trust others, to form healthy relationships, and to speak out about my experiences. It has also meant taking care of myself, both physically and emotionally, and finding healthy coping mechanisms to deal with the difficult moments.

Finding meaning in the journey of sexual abuse has been another important aspect of my healing process. It has meant recognizing that my experiences have shaped who I am today, but that they do not define me. It has meant seeking out positive experiences and relationships, and finding ways to give back to others who have experienced similar traumas.

Through my journey of healing, I have also found a sense of purpose in advocating for survivors of sexual abuse. By sharing my story and raising awareness about the impact of sexual abuse, I hope to inspire others to seek help, find healing, and find their own sense of resilience and purpose. While the journey of healing from sexual abuse is not an easy one, it is one that can lead to a sense of empowerment and strength, and I am grateful for the opportunity to continue to grow and learn from my experiences.

YOU ARE NOT ALONE

Never make the mistake of thinking you are alone in this healing journey.

I understand how difficult it can be to speak out and seek help, but I want to encourage you to take that first step. I want to assure you that seeking help is not a sign of weakness. It takes incredible strength and courage to acknowledge what has happened and to begin the process of healing.

Be kind and patient with yourself. Healing is not a linear process, and there may be setbacks along the way. But with time, support, and perseverance, you can learn to cope with the impact of the abuse and find a path towards healing and recovery. Remember that you are not alone and that healing is possible. You deserve to live a life free from the impact of sexual abuse.

Hanna Olivas

Founder and CEO of She Rises Studios

<https://www.linkedin.com/company/she-rises-studios/>
<https://www.instagram.com/sherisesstudios>
<https://www.facebook.com/sherisesstudios>
www.SheRisesStudios.com

Author, Speaker, and Founder. Hanna was born and raised in Las Vegas, Nevada, and has paved her way to becoming one of the most influential women of 2023. Hanna is the co-founder of She Rises Studios and the founder of the Brave & Beautiful Blood Cancer Foundation. Her journey started in 2017 when she was first diagnosed with Multiple Myeloma, an incurable blood cancer. Now more than ever, her focus is to empower other women to become leaders because The Future is Female. She is currently traveling and speaking publicly to women to educate them on entrepreneurship, leadership, and owning the female power within.

FAITH OF A MUSTARD SEED

By Hanna Olivas

I woke up this morning with a sense of purpose, knowing that today is the day I will finally begin to tell my story. A story that has been weighing on me for far too long but one that I know needs to be said. My name is Hanna Olivas, and this is my journey of healing.

When I was younger, I never thought I would be a victim of sexual assault. I always felt that I was invincible, that nothing wrong could ever happen to me. But that all changed in the blink of an eye at a very young age. I was sexually molested by my mother's boyfriends at the age of two and three years old, in my teens, and again by my ex-husband.

It's hard to describe the feelings I experienced in the aftermath of the assault. I felt violated, ashamed, and completely alone. I didn't tell anyone what had happened for a long time, not even my closest friends or family. I thought it would go away if I just pushed it down and tried to forget about it. But it didn't. It lingered like a dark cloud hanging over my head.

It wasn't until the Me Too movement gained momentum that I began to feel like I could talk about what had happened to me. Watching other women come forward with their stories made me feel less alone, giving me the courage to speak out. I wrote a blog post and book about my experience and was overwhelmed by the outpouring of support that I received from friends and strangers alike.

But even with all of the support, I still felt like I was stuck. I was stuck in the trauma of what had happened to me, and I didn't know how to move forward. That's when I decided to seek out therapy. It was a hard decision, but it was one of the best decisions I have ever made. I could confront the trauma through therapy and begin to work through it.

It wasn't easy, and sometimes I felt like giving up. But I kept going, and slowly but surely, I began to see progress. I started to feel like myself again, like I could move on from what had happened to me. And now, years later, I can confidently say that I am healed. I am still a work in progress, but I am no longer defined by the trauma that once consumed me.

If there's one thing I've learned on this journey, it's that healing is possible. It's not easy and takes time, but it's possible. And if my story can inspire even one person to seek help and begin their healing journey, it will have all been worth it. Me too, but never again.

Healing is a word that is used so often, and I wonder if people realize and understand the actual meaning and how to become fully healed. Especially when the hurt or damage is so deep within. As you read this chapter, I pray you to find your inner peace and healing. I have found my healing comes from three places, Faith, Forgiveness, and Love.

Let's talk about faith first. Being a victim of sexual abuse, I often questioned, "Why me?"

"Why would God allow such evil and devious acts to happen to one of his own children?"

The answers came in waves. We all face trials and tribulations; however, it's what we do within the storm and what we learn from it. There were times I spent a lot of nights alone in tears asking God to take me, to make the pain and abuse stop. I spent years being sexually molested and abused. I felt dirty, marked, and damaged beyond repair. I was constantly living in fear and anger. From time to time, I would feel as if there was a glimpse of hope ahead for me. I always have said and believed, " The faith of a mustard can turn into a garden of hope, healing, and opportunities." Faith is an incredible gift we are all born with. We just have to develop our faith and know that we are not defined by our circumstances, and we can begin a new life healed, happy, and healthy. Part of healing from trauma also requires forgiveness of ourselves. Sometimes we blame ourselves for what happened and believe we caused it, which is not valid.

The perpetrator is the person responsible for the abuse; we've done nothing to deserve that. I hope you realize that in your healing journey. Most would say it's impossible to forgive such an act and the person who carries it out. However, in order to heal, we must forgive ourselves and focus on how to move forward.

Forgiveness is a complex topic to discuss, especially when it comes to sexual abuse. It is essential to acknowledge the complexity and sensitivity of this issue and to approach the subject with empathy, compassion, and understanding. Here are some tips on how to talk about forgiveness in the context of sexual abuse:

1. Acknowledge the severity of the abuse: Sexual abuse is a traumatic experience that can have a profound impact on a survivor's life. It is important to acknowledge the seriousness of the abuse and the pain and trauma that the survivor has experienced.

2. Emphasize that forgiveness is a personal choice: Forgiveness is a personal choice that should never be forced or coerced. It is up to the survivor to decide whether or not they are ready to forgive the perpetrator.

3. Recognize that forgiveness is not a requirement for healing: Forgiveness is not a requirement for healing from sexual abuse. It is possible to heal and move forward without forgiving the perpetrator.

4. Discuss the potential benefits of forgiveness: Forgiveness can have many benefits, including improved mental and physical

health, greater happiness, and stronger relationships. However, it is important to emphasize that forgiveness is not necessary to experience these benefits.

5. Encourage survivors to prioritize their own healing: Healing from sexual abuse should be the survivor's top priority. It is important to encourage survivors to prioritize their own recovery and to seek out resources and support that can help them on their journey.

6. Validate survivors' feelings and experiences: Survivors may experience a wide range of emotions, including anger, sadness, and shame. It is important to validate these feelings and experiences and to provide a safe and supportive space for survivors to share their stories and work through their emotions.

7. Highlight the importance of boundaries: Forgiveness does not mean that survivors have to reconcile with their abuser or allow them back into their lives. It is essential to emphasize the importance of boundaries and to support survivors in setting and maintaining boundaries that protect their safety and well-being. Next, let's focus on Self Love. I think we lose it when we're defiled. We hate ourselves, and many of us go into self-destruction mode, which only leads to more pain for us. I went down a deep dark rabbit hole for years with drinking and wrong choices. I really had to learn how to love myself and the new version of myself. Here are a few ways I was able to accomplish that in my healing journey.

Finding self-love after experiencing sexual abuse can be a difficult and complex process. It is important to approach this topic with sensitivity, empathy, and compassion. Here are some tips on how to talk about finding self-love after sexual abuse:

One of the most effective ways of finding self-love after sexual abuse is by talking about it with someone you trust. This could be a family member, friend, counselor, or therapist specializing in trauma recovery. Talking openly and honestly can help you process your emotions and start accepting what has happened, and move forward in your life. It's also important to remember that healing takes time – there's no rush, and you should take as long as necessary to find peace within yourself again.

Another way of finding self-love after sexual abuse is by being kind to yourself - both physically and mentally - every day. This could involve taking some time out, eating healthily, getting enough sleep, or exercising regularly – whatever works for you! It's also important to practice positive thinking – try writing down three things that make you happy each day or focus on the good rather than the bad things. Learning how to love yourself again is key because it allows you to build up your resilience moving forward, empowering you in many aspects of life, including relationships, work, etc.

Finally, seeking out support groups or organizations can be a great way of finding self-love after sexual abuse too! There are many options available online or even locally, depending on where you live, which offer various forms of support such as group therapy sessions or one-to-one counseling sessions specifically geared towards helping survivors overcome their trauma-related issues such as self-esteem issues etc. Getting involved with these types of activities can really help give survivors back their voice and control over their lives again!

Finding self-love after experiencing sexual abuse doesn't happen overnight, but it is possible with patience, understanding, and compassion toward oneself! Hopefully, with these tips, anyone affected by this kind of trauma can start rebuilding their confidence slowly but surely so they can look forward positively to the future again.

Over the years of my healing journey, I know three things to be true: Faith, Love, and Forgiveness go hand in hand. As I've written my second Me Too But Never Again book, I've grown so much, and I no longer feel like that marked dirty girl. I live a beautiful life and have a wonderful family and support system. Although my abusers were my mother's boyfriends, a teenage friend, and my ex-husband and father of my children, I can genuinely say I have let go and moved past so much of the pain. That's what I want for you. Please never give up on your healing or yourself. You are worthy and loved. You are not alone. Speak out and tell your truth. Find the support system that works for you. Don't be afraid to tell! With all my love, we are Me Too But Never Again.

Xoxo,
Hanna Olivas

Kyla Biedermann

Legacy Women Affiliates LLC

https://www.facebook.com/kyla.biedermann.5/
https://www.instagram.com/thekyla.b/
https://linktr.ee/kylabiedermann

Born and raised in Fredericksburg Texas, Kyla Biedermann is an international bestselling author in the anthology, Shattering the stigma of single motherhood, a speaker, teacher, and veteran; owner and founder of Legacy Women Affiliates and a member of the She Rises Studios leadership team. She served 8 years in the Navy as a Cryptologic Technician. After becoming a single mother to her son in 2020 she realized the attitudes and culture surrounding single motherhood needed to change, starting with her own. This began a long journey of self-development and education in pursuit of finding answers and healing. Kyla's motto in life is, Always Learning, Always Growing, Always Changing. Through Legacy Women Affiliates she builds and supports Legacy women, and advocates for mental health and against domestic violence. In her free time, she enjoys spending time with her son, true crime documentaries, shopping, history, politics, and staying healthy physical, mentally, and spiritually.

MILITARY SEXUAL TRAUMA

By Kyla Biedermann

Toxic Behaviors

In 2018, around my six years mark in the Navy, I was assigned to the USS Momsen DDG-92, which would very quickly become my assignment to hell on earth. By the end of the first week, I was sat down by my new supervisor to let me know that there was already a rumor going around the ship about me. Apparently within a few short days I had sex with all the men in another division, approximately 5-7 men. Rumors are a terrible thing in the military, I was very used to having rumors go around about me, especially every time I was new to a command, and of course, I had heard the rumors about other women, but this was a whole new level for me. I believe it was at this point I lost all credibility on this vessel, regardless of the last 6 years I had spent as an outstanding sailor, regardless that I didn't even know the names of the men I was being accused of sleeping with, regardless of who I really was- I would now and forever on be known as, "That new E-5 that will sleep with anyone" to all current and future sailors. Those initial rumors they *heard,* or their *initial observations* as they come into contact with you throughout the ship in passing, no matter how ignorant, factless and baseless they are, spread like wildfire, and whatever catches fire in the beginning is very hard to put out when there is one you versus three hundred other sailors, who can't help but hear and then believe the rumors about you. This was the very beginning of my experience of hell on earth.

Toxic Leadership

A couple of months later, I met a guy on the ship. We had a mutual interest in each other, and at this time we were underway more than we were home so we would hang out on the ship and talk when we had a chance to and we would also hang out with each other when we hit port. At the time I had tested for E-6 and was awaiting results. This individual was an E-6 and we were in completely different departments, so I was not speaking to someone in my chain of command, nor someone that had any kind of effect on my evaluations, therefore I felt secure that I was doing the right thing and we were not breaking any rules. Little did I know, the Chief's Mess on this ship had been actively looking for a reason to go after this guy because he had been dating a low-ranking sailor right up to the point we had begun talking, literally as soon as I came into the picture, they lunged at the opportunity to charge him using a female they cared nothing about. Two weeks into us getting to know each other, we were scheduled for a disciplinary review board, DRB for short, charged with fraternization. DRBs are held by the Chief's Mess to gather and review information on crimes possibly committed-usually known for chiefs yelling and cursing at sailors to intimidate them-if found guilty after this non-judiciary review process, you then go on to what is called XOI, where the information is presented before the Executive Officer of the ship, who will decide to pass you off to the commanding officer for Captain's mast or can also drop the case at that point.

Before my DRB it was made perfectly clear to me that this case was not necessarily about me, I just needed to go in there and tell the truth about everything and it would be dropped for me. My DRB consisted of approximately 30-40 male Chiefs ranging in age from approximately 28-40 years of age, not a single woman Chief, and all Chiefs from the air detachment that was currently embarked were invited to join the escapade, none of whom I had never met before, were not familiar with me as a sailor whatsoever, and were not part of the ship's company. I stood there, all alone, at attention in my dress white uniform, whole body shaking, scared out of my mind, and answering their questions with 100% honesty because my career was on the line and I just wanted this to be over with, until the questions began to go in one certain direction. CMDMC, "CTT2, is it true that you had sex in the back seat of a Volkswagen beetle?" I was horrified and confused. Why was this was coming up? I would understand if I had committed a sexual act on the ship, or in an unauthorized location on base, but that was not the case, and this question was completely out of line. I stayed quiet. I had no idea what to say at first. The CMC and all the other chiefs were almost leaning in, giddy to hear my answer. Finally, I spoke, "No," I replied, thinking we would move on to the rest of the questions, and refusing to entertain that kind of conversation, especially as a young woman in a room full of older men. Not one single chief believed this was inappropriate or even out of the scope of the investigation, even after what happened next because they all stayed quiet and let this unfold however their leader, CMC decided to proceed. He then made it clear he knew I was lying, despite any proof. He only believed what he had heard and went on to let me know how terrible it was that I would not discuss my personal sexual life. Then another chief and another chief all were pleading with me to just tell the truth so everything would be ok and we could all just move on. Even an air detachment Chief, who began his speech with how he didn't know me and I didn't know him but I needed to tell the truth about this because when he had indulged in an affair on his wife as a chief and was caught, he told the truth and it saved his career. I finally broke, "Okay, yes I did." That was all I could say as I began to tear up from the frustration and humiliation, and just like they said, it all stopped there. That's all they really wanted to know. Master Chief then informed me of my charges and that he was adding lying and adultery to them and would see me at XOI.

At my XOI, the executive officer kept all charges and let me know that he would be looking into revoking my top-secret clearance because I was a liar, and he would be sending me to Captain's mast. In these nonjudicial hearings, there is no innocent until proven guilty. Even if you are innocent, they can make you guilty of whatever they so choose. I did the only thing I could bring myself to do: I wrote a letter to the Captain detailing every moment of this process so far including the sexual harassment I had endured at the hands of the Chief's Mess, I reiterated that I was a good sailor and if she just looked at any evaluation I had so far, she would see that I was a high performing, motivated sailor and would never do anything I thought would hurt my career, and listed all the reasons I believed I was following all Naval guidelines while getting to know this individual. I had to fight for my career. I had personally never seen a captain drop charges, so I knew at the very least I was preparing for restriction, which is confinement on the ship. At the end of the day when everyone else goes home to their families, you stay on the ship and continue to work, your cell phone is confiscated and you essentially are a prisoner for at least 30 days. This will usually also be accompanied by a reduction in pay and even rank in more serious cases. I was being accused of some serious crimes, and knew I was easily facing all three of these punishments.

The captain ended up dropping all charges for both of us, I believe she did the right thing and I thank her for her strength, fairness, consideration, and leadership that day. It should have never got to that point though, and there are too many other sailors who have had their lives and careers unfairly and unjustly affected because of corrupt leadership. This is why I am dedicated to healing myself and others who are living with trauma caused by poor leadership in the military and speaking out about how we can turn this around and make the military a better place for everyone. Leaders in the Navy are treated like demigods and allowed to wreak havoc on their junior sailors however they like, and everyone just goes along with it. There is a huge lack of moral and ethical leadership, which continues to breed toxicity and cause destruction and trauma to the human beings that are the victims of this lawlessness. We have the technology and resources to turn this around. It might not be an overnight thing, but this cannot be achieved without a willingness to change, holding each other accountable, and action towards tearing down the very framework that is allowing and feeding the toxicity.

What is Trauma and How to Navigate Through It

Some individuals might not be in a place where they can begin to receive and implement this information. Grief is not an easy process, and most will experience the following five stages: denial, anger, bargaining, depression, and acceptance. It is important to know where you stand and allow yourself proper time to work through your grief. There is a time and a place for everything and right now may not be the time for some to hear, understand and implement more complex or advanced healing techniques and that is okay. Take your time to get to the point where you are ready to begin asserting effort towards further healing.

No matter what we have been through, we all have one thing in common and that is, we experienced trauma. Trauma is an attack on our nervous system that results in many different side effects that vary per person but fall into four main categories: physical, such as fatigue and digestive issues; cognitive, which are intellectual activities for example flashbacks, nightmares, and memory loss; behavioral, including social isolation and lack of interest; lastly, psychological and examples of that are depression, anxiety and feelings of guilt, shame, and hopelessness. There are many more examples per category and I highly advise those who are working on healing to investigate all the different side effects and identify which ones might be affecting you, and then you can really move forward in finding personal solutions and healing techniques. As cliché as it sounds, I want to reiterate that healing from grief is a process and there are steps to getting where you would like to be, *you cannot recover from it until you get through it.*

Cognitive Decline

When experiencing the side effects of trauma, a common response is to shut down. When shut down or slowdown of brain activity happens, it impairs cognitive performance. For example, it takes less effort for a brain to think negatively than it does for a brain to think positively. Therefore, when the brain is allowed to constantly wallow in negativity and never worked out to think positively, or when the brain stops learning on a regular basis, it will begin to experience cognitive decline. In other words. when the brain is not used in the same capacity it once was, it experiences decline, and it is much easier to continue to decline than it is to fight back, take control of the brain, and begin working that muscle out again. This is why you hear, "Change your mind, change your life." Look for the lessons during the hard times. Yes, we went through trauma, but there is so much we can learn about ourselves through that, and there is so much to learn about healing, forgiveness, being happy again, how to grow as a person, how to be more in control of yourself, and how people treat you. We will never be perfect, but we can always learn and improve ourselves. This is not the end, and we can still live a beautiful and happy life after trauma. You have to choose that for yourself though, and then take action and not let yourself decline.

Identity Crisis

The military is famously known for breaking you down so they can build you back up, but through that process self-identity is lost, and when too much of yourself is lost, the effects can be deadly. An identity crisis will make you ask yourself, "Who am I? What are my passions? What is my purpose?" You may wonder why everything in your life sucks, why don't you have control when you feel like you should, and on and on. Not having proper boundaries set in the proper areas results in an identity crisis. There are seven areas of our lives that require proper attention and maintenance or boundaries: physical, emotional, intellectual, time, financial, spiritual, and sexual. These boundaries keep us moving forward in a positive direction, help us define ourselves, and allow us to maintain safe internal and external environments. Most of our boundaries are learned from observations during childhood. Children are not aware that they might be inheriting bad habits or boundaries at all or until it is too late. This is why children that grow up with parents that divorce are more likely to end up divorced, children with abusive parents often end up exhibiting abusive tendencies as adults, and passive agressive parents will usually have passive aggressive children. Time, financial, and social habits that have negative side effects may run in the family. Whatever it may be, that chaos in your life will continue to happen and have a lot to do with who you are, how you were raised, and what your priorities are. Healing and growth can only happen when you have identified where you are going wrong. Take responsibility for your role in the chaos and commit to learning and implementing healthier boundaries and habits. The more you define boundaries in each category by learning what healthy boundaries and actions look like, the more you learn about yourself, the more you define yourself, the more you find things that are for you and the more you push away those things that are not for you. The more you learn and grow the more you work out your brain, and the healthier your brain is the healthier the rest of you will be, and your family and social circles will improve as well!

Lisa Brennan

Self Love Empowerment Relationship Coach and Spiritual Mentor

https://www.facebook.com/lisa.brennankew

Hi I'm Lisa Brennan,

When a person is uncertain of their feelings for you, you become uncertain of yourself. Sadly, millions of people can't ask someone to "love me for me."

I'm a self-love coach who empowers you to heal your love story. We are taught by society to love and honor those that we love, and that staying together should be something to be celebrated. Love is beautiful and it should be celebrated, but we need to ask what is the depths and loyalty of love?

You are not less of a person for walking away from someone who hurt you. Letting go of emotional attachments is not a sign of weakness, it's a sign of strength and courage.

It's not about forgetting the painful event happened. It's moving on and remembering who you were before the world tried to convince you otherwise.

It reminds you each day of the love and respect that you have for yourself.

That's beautiful; you always were, and always will be enough.

THE GIRL BEHIND THE SMILE

By Lisa Brennan

Every birthday candle I blew out or falling star I have seen for as long as I can remember, I always wished for love, true happiness, and inner peace. My sensitive heart felt more like a curse than it did a blessing.

We all have something we hide from the world; I hid my painful past behind my smile.

When a person doesn't get their emotional needs met at a young age, they often chase the high of love. Unconsciously, they are chasing out the low of their insecurities and expecting a different ending. It never works out as planned.

I became addicted to unhealthy relationships. I was codependent on my partners to make me happy. I lacked personal boundaries because, well, not having them felt more like home. It was an open invitation to add conditions to the love they gave me and fill my life with self-sacrifices.

We always say, 'I'm falling in love with you," but I believe we should rephrase it to, "I'm rising in love with you." Doesn't that sound more like love to you?

Throughout my life I had lessons wrapped in sandpaper. They were rough. I was betrayed up, down, and sideways. My heart and confidence were shattered. One part of me was emotional, with so much love to give, and the other part was numb. You can't clip a woman's wings and still expect her to be your angel and raise you higher.

As men fell in love with my looks, big heart, and free-spirited personality, I, on the other hand, was falling out of love with myself.

All I ever wanted was for someone's arms to feel like a safe haven, someone who saw my scars as beautiful. Proof that I fought the battle I never wanted or asked for, so I could stop fighting so hard to prove my worth.

The million-dollar question I asked myself was, "Will I ever be able to forgive, and will my heart ever recover?"

Wouldn't it be nice if chemistry made love last? Lust can blindside you, but a person's true colors always shine through.

As a lovestruck, naïve high school dropout and teenage mom, I thought my first husband's jealousy meant that "he loves me." All it took was that first hit, when my daughter was only three months old, to understand that relationships don't always end up with a beautiful love story. The broken promise that stung the most was, "I'll never hurt you again."

Making sure I was only his, he manipulated me. "You can't have friends, Lisa, you're a mom now." I wanted to be the runaway bride! Each time I attempted to leave, he threatened to take the children away. We moved out of state several times, and my sister made the five-hour trip many times to come to my rescue. Restraining orders were a joke!

My final goodbye gift was the words, "If you leave me, you'll never see a red cent." Ironically, it was the one promise he did keep. During my 12 years of marriage, I had wanted a partner in crime, not to feel as if my mind was being controlled. People do change, we did, but I needed him then.

Domestic violence robbed my daughter and son of their dad. They had to grow up faster than what I hoped for. Sadly, I knew what that felt like. I smiled even though my heart was aching. How was I going to survive? I got my GED, waitressed, and my mom helped when she could. Barely holding on by a thread, I prayed, "Please give me a sign."

My prayers were answered when I met my second husband who was older and wealthier. He wanted a beautiful wife, and I wanted a beautiful life.

I moved to Illinois, and I blended in with the elite. The affluent Chicago suburb made me feel like a Princess. We traveled the world, and it was everything I ever dreamed of. I was happy that my family was creating new memories. My children were in the best schools. I didn't work, his choice. I was grateful for the opportunity to attend college in my 30s because it held the promise of independence. This was the life I couldn't give them on my own.

We were finally stable. Was this too good to be true? I was waiting for the shoe to drop—it did.

At the time, the word narcissist wasn't in my vocabulary. It was a camouflaged red flag, with him being the good guy. Our first fight was about how much money I spent shopping. I felt confused when I was punished and put on an allowance. Was I his wife, trophy wife, or his daughter?

He pacified me by saying, "I work hard for our money, and I've got plans for us, honey." It made me feel guilty and obligated. Then I became angry. He honestly believed he'd saved a small-town woman and made me feel small-minded when he arrogantly asked, "Where would you be without out me?" WHAT? After all I had done for him? I'd cry and he'd coddle me. It was a vicious cycle.

Eventually, my husband's insecurities led to obsession and control, "Lisa, you can't have single friends, they think differently, who's going to watch you?" I wanted to be invisible as he pulled me off the dance floor. It was deja vu. I loved him, but I lost respect for him.

Hearing my children scream, "You're not my dad!" tore my heart in two. I knew that I had sacrificed my happiness. When I finally had the courage to leave, I was shocked to discover he had taken me off the bank account! Vacations and medication just numbed my reality.

It's hard to get by in life with just a smile. Sadly, I didn't recognize the woman I was pretending to be. Feeling trapped and heartbroken, I couldn't think clearly; I had suicidal ideations.

My daughter held my hand and told me, "Mom, I would be so devastated if you never found true love because, out of everyone in the world, you deserve it." Tears are the words a heart can't express. I could no longer hold them back. Her hug felt like heaven replying, "Me too."

I asked for a divorce, but he just said, "Let's get away, just you and me, we can work this out." It felt like a bribe.

My lawyer said, "You'd be better off staying with him," and I replied, "You marry him!" Our marriage was a lie. He was hiding money and the title of our beautiful home was in his daughter's name. I received less than I did from a car accident settlement. We both made mistakes, but is that what fourteen years of my love is worth?—Ouch!

He paid for my Bachelor's degree in Psychology, but really, I got a master's degree in life!

I was happy to be free and built back my confidence. Although I learned the hard way that time does not heal; your perception of yourself heals. Empaths are easy targets for narcissists, especially ones with unresolved pain.

I fell prey to a ruthless evil narcissist. He gained my confidence, promising me a great life. You'd think I'd learn! He conned me out of money and stole my identity. I was devastated and mortified when I was sued by three companies for $118,000. He even threatened me with a sex tape so I wouldn't go to the police.

I was not his only victim; he had a girlfriend the entire time and many fell for his charm. Nauseated and in disbelief, I screamed, "Why me?" Please have mercy on my heart." Five months felt like five years in hell. But karma is a bitch, and he did go to jail.

Enough was FINALLY enough!

My loved ones and my faith were my lifelines. Broke, I moved back to Wisconsin, leaving behind my adult children, grandchildren, and friends. At the time, I questioned my sanity. Was I that desperate for love and acceptance that I would devalue my worth? I was in fight or flight. if I continued at that rate, the toll it would take on my mind and body would be catastrophic!

I fell on hard times. How did I get here?

Society says we should take responsibility for our life. That's hard to ask of someone who's been through trauma, It's the main reason many remain hidden behind their mask of shame, instead of remaining true to themselves.

In life, some things are out of your control. Growing up, I had to walk on eggshells around my abusive alcoholic stepfather. The moment I knew no one would save me was when I looked into my mama's eyes as she stood there frozen like a deer in the headlights as my stepfather made a sarcastic cruel joke about my freckles, saying they were fly shit! He was the only one laughing. My mouth dropped, but no words came out.

I hated hearing them argue. In the morning, everyone pretended nothing happened the night before. We were all victims. The word empath was foreign to me; all I knew was that I felt my mama's and siblings' pain. I am dyslexic, and instead of making me feel good about myself, my stepfather called me a "dingbat" for getting things wrong. At school, I was liked, but I wasn't considered the "cool" girl. I was too embarrassed to bring friends home.

We weren't poor, but we weren't rich either. Mama worked nights; I craved her attention. I faked being sick and skipped school just to spend time with her. Those were cherished moments. Watching her get ready for work, I would beg, "Please stay." Her sweet voice always responded with, "Don't you want nice things?" Yes, but I wanted and needed her more.

I wished I could spend more time with my daddy, but my parents didn't get along. In his mind, he thought we had a better life. The weekend visits became less frequent. If he only knew.

But things kept getting worse!

Frightened in my pink Barbie nightgown, I knew what was about to happen as, once again, my stepfather crept back into my room. I had slowly faded away as my mind and my body were no longer mine to own before I even had my first real kiss. My boundary lines were blurred. Full of guilt and shame, I internalized what happened to me as my fault. My "secret" was safe with me.

There were many red flags. A school counselor asked, concerned, "Is everything okay at home?" I lied and said, "I'm fine" I was not FINE! When I bravely told them what was happening, I went to live with a relative, but it turned out to be another nightmare. I was bullied, and I dropped out of high school.

Today, I can clearly see that my mom and dad loved me very much. I loved them, but I was angry and hurt. I'm sure that my parents had their own generational wounds passed down to them, but in those days people did not ask about family affairs. Behind closed doors, my family developed patterns of codependency. They did the best they could and both apologized.

Regardless, it left deep wounds on our souls.

If I had been brave enough to say something sooner, would I have felt the need to search for something lovable, beautiful, and smart about myself? Would I have been physically, verbally, and sexually abused? Would I not have sabotaged my chance at having healthy loving relationships, success, and happiness? Patterns are hard to break. How could I ask my partners to love me properly when deep down I couldn't love myself?

One day can change a person's entire life. Two months before my 50th birthday, my entire world fell apart, but the catalyst of pain was the need for a breakthrough. First, I was forced to let go of my mom's hand as she lost the fight to beat pancreatic cancer. She always wanted me to be happy. I would give anything for one more hug and to hear her voice. She's my guardian angel.

Two months after my mom's death, the unthinkable happened, I was knocking on heaven's door, fighting for MY life! The surgeons claim that it's a miracle that I'm alive.

Twenty years prior, after a serious car accident, a metal frame was installed in my neck. It got infected. The structure began to come apart and punctured a hole in my throat, causing my lungs to aspirate. My head was half–shaven and 36 staples were inserted in the back of my head. The front of my neck looked like I was in a knife fight. I was placed on a feeding tube. My weight dropped to 96 pounds.

When you're at your lowest, the people who truly matter become crystal clear. Many were by my side, but my sister was my rock.

67 days of recovering from my injuries in a rehabilitation center allowed me time to think about my life. My ego struggled with exactly how much external validation I needed. What did I have to lose? I found the courage to surrender and go deep for the answers. I let go of what tethered me down—my hunted past full of shame.

I drowned out the cries of "Nurse, nurse, help me" from those suffering as I listened to spiritual meditation. My guides walked me through the process of transformation. In awe, visions of both my parents who passed away and Jesus appeared before my mind's eye. I am forever grateful. Pain can cover the wounds permanently, but it may leave you in darkness or love and faith can be the healing guiding light.

Today, I'm an Intuitive Relationship Coach and spiritual mentor. I received training on how to release trauma. Discovering patterns of attachment styles to love and clearing emotional blocks, as well as clearing the negative energy of the body helps manage triggers and provides you with the confidence and self-worth to attract healthy love into your life.

Many that are at a crossroads in their life say, "I feel lost, or I feel broken" There's something missing, or a nagging feeling of wanting more. That's your soul guiding you to be authentic.

When you chase peace, it comes with a lot of goodbyes. Being authentic is the heartfelt willingness to be vulnerable and accept the unedited version of your story. This means remaining true to your personality, values, and standards. When you silence your deepest fears, you rise your moods and vibrations. You can see other's intentions more clearly, therefore protecting your heart.

My heart was once full of broken promises, but now I promise to never break my own. Self-love is not selfish, it's a healthy spirit. Everyone who tried to take my power away encouraged me to empower myself.

I found someone I never want to lose again and that's ME.

—Self-Love Empowerment Relationship Coach and Spiritual Mentor, Lisa Brennan

Melanie Starr

https://www.linkedin.com/in/melanie-starr-87850813/
https://www.facebook.com/healbraveandstrong
www.empoweryourpotential.ca

Melanie Starr is a holistic wellness practitioner and coach whose perspective is rooted in science as much as spirituality. She has been a consultant and writer in the medical field for more than 25 years, while pursuing her own deep healing through yoga, energy therapy and many other practices that engage the body, breath, heart, mind and soul in the vital work of personal development.

Melanie is a long-time yoga teacher, certified Master Emotional Freedom Techniques (EFT) practitioner, Reiki Master-Teacher, and certified practitioner of Integrated Energy Therapy® and Soul Realignment®. She is a recipient of a 2023 Woman on Fire Award in recognition of her work helping women heal trauma, release fear and shame, build resiliency, and claim emotional freedom.

Melanie offers one-on-one and group programs in such areas as healing childhood trauma, fostering self-esteem, creating healthy relationships, and turning your divorce into the best thing that ever happened to you.

YOU ARE WORTHY AND YOU CAN HEAL FROM CHILDHOOD SEXUAL ABUSE

By Melanie Starr

It feels very strange to finally write this story. After more than 25 years as a professional writer, I have never written my own story. I've always shone the spotlight on others and told their stories, preferring to stay in the shadows myself.

It makes sense, because I always felt I had something to hide and carried a heavy secret in my heart: the painful truth that I was sexually abused as a very young child. This made me feel unworthy for years, although I overcompensated with a neurotic focus on making the highest marks, being the hardest-working employee, the most self-sacrificing mother, you name it. Proving myself to myself and others was how I coped with my inner turmoil and shame.

When the #MeToo movement took off in 2017, I remained silent, still unable to speak, even though I had definitely been sexually harassed in the workplace. In addition to the abusively long hours, it was the creepy comments, lecherous leers, and trespassing touches from my male clients that drove me out of my fledgling PR career in the early 1990s.

But why did I feel so bad about sexual innuendo and energy directed my way by such immature men? Why couldn't I just send them a sharp retort to burst their slimy balloons? Why did I shrink inside, lose my voice, and ultimately run away?

Now that I have been working for a number of years as a practitioner and coach helping women heal trauma, build resiliency, and claim emotional freedom, I know why. Now that I understand how the nervous system works, how early trauma imprints itself on the deepest levels of our being, and how trauma patterns repeat themselves, I know why I abandoned myself in those flustering moments and handed my power away.

And that is why I am finally ready to share my story. I want to help anyone else who struggles to stand up for themselves, speak their truth, set clear boundaries, own their worth, and pursue their potential. Once you understand how trauma plays out in your nervous system and makes you feel blocked and limited in your life, you have the opportunity to change it. Awareness is the beginning, followed by knowledge, tools, and dedicated practice. I can only scratch the surface in this short chapter, but I teach this material in depth in my healing programs.

This chapter deals primarily with childhood sexual abuse, an original wound that sets the template for continued abuse. Before I dive in, I must point out that ANY abuse in childhood—it does not have to be sexual—sets that child up for a lifetime of disempowerment and abuse that can land in many forms, including emotional, physical, verbal, financial, and sexual abuse. And children can be traumatized by things far less severe than abuse. Having a manipulative mother or unavailable father can be enough to put trauma patterns in place, as I have seen again and again in my work with women struggling to recover from codependency, toxic relationships, and midlife divorce.

That said, childhood sexual abuse is shockingly, tragically common. According to the World Health Organization (WHO), one in five girls and one in 13 boys is sexually abused before age 17. But studies of adult survivors show nearly half of children who are victimized NEVER disclose the abuse. I don't know if the WHO statistics reflect this non-disclosure, so it is entirely possible the actual percentages are much higher. As much as it is #MeToo, it is quite possibly #YouToo if you are female and reading this book.

So this isn't really about me, it's about everyone who's had their innocence and power stolen when they were too young to defend themselves and/or even understand what was happening. Research shows more than 90 percent of children who are sexually abused know the abuser well, so their trust is being abused along with their body, leaving them filled with confusion and fear.

Now you might be thinking, "What happened to me wasn't THAT bad. It was just the kid down the street feeling me up and making me suck his dick." But if you felt uneasy, squeamish, confused, scared, ashamed, trapped, forced, manipulated, or any other bad-feeling emotion, you were negatively impacted.

We tend to minimize our own traumas, to tell ourselves we haven't faced anything as terrible as others, and this is often true. But it doesn't mean we should disown our pain. This doesn't help us to heal. In fact, it can traumatize us further. I want you to know that even if what happened to you wasn't the worst thing you've ever heard, it hurt you, and your pain matters.

In my case, it was an adolescent boy in the neighbourhood who managed to isolate, corner, intimidate and coerce me on multiple occasions when I was five and six years old. He threatened me with physical punishment if I dared say a word, rapping me sharply on the head with his knuckles to make his point clear. The incidents left me feeling anxious, unsafe, and so ashamed of being overpowered that I wanted to hide from God.

Shame is the most toxic and damaging emotion, as it is not so much the sense that we have DONE something wrong but rather that we ARE inherently wrong in our being.

Shame drives us to hide from the world and feel unworthy of receiving good things and maybe even that we deserve bad things. My buried shame led me to punish myself for years through my ruthless inner critic, which never allowed me to feel that I measured up. Pangs of shame would sear through my whole body, and I would berate myself anytime I said or did anything that wasn't "perfect," repeating the terrible mantra, "I hate myself, I hate myself," under my breath and sometimes even out loud. Only in the last 10 years have I silenced that voice. I'm 56, so it was a long time spent hating myself.

Those incidents in my early childhood pushed me into my first experiences of the trauma freeze response. If something like this happened to you when you were a child, it is highly likely that you also experienced the freeze response.

You are probably familiar with the stress response known as "fight or flight": when you are in a threatening situation and you feel the strong urge to fight back or run away. But when you don't have that option—because the person threatening you is too big to fight and too fast to flee—it's too much for your nervous system, and you go instantly into the freeze response. This is a paralyzing state not unlike "playing dead," as many animals do in a last-ditch attempt to escape the jaws of a predator. You can't move, you can't think, and you can't speak.

What is particularly awful for a child—or anyone—who has gone into freeze mode in response to a sexual invasion is that, later, they can't understand why they didn't say or do anything to protect themselves or escape. These thoughts add to their internalized sense of shame, guilt, and confusion and may be used by the abuser as evidence of consent and a tool for further manipulation of the victim.

Having gone into fight, flight, and freeze once, your nervous system is now primed to trigger back into the stress and trauma responses with even less stimulus in the future, creating a pattern that tends to repeat. This dysregulation can leave you much more vulnerable to all sorts of bullying, not to mention extreme anxiety as a day-to-day state.

Adding to the damage is the fact that, prior to age seven, children operate in the brainwave state known as theta, a highly suggestible, dreamlike state that adults enter in light sleep, deep relaxation, and hypnosis. Children's brains do not generate the beta waves that allow critical thinking, so whatever is said and done to them goes straight into their subconscious minds as if they were under hypnosis. This is the subconscious programming that will then drive the majority of their reactions and behaviours for life.

What children learn deeply in those moments of abuse is that they don't have the right to boundaries. Others can transgress upon them, and they have no recourse. And they feel "wrong" because their instinctive sense that what's happening is wrong gets overridden by someone more powerful, and now they doubt their own instincts. This cuts them off from their "gut feelings," so they are less able to detect and assess danger in the future.

The double and triple whammy is that now their bodies are a frightening or confusing place. Still, they can't even escape in their heads because they don't have the intellectual capacity to rationalize what happened and assign the blame where it belongs: to the perpetrator. It's a "nowhere to run, nowhere to hide" scenario that can keep them in a prolonged stress or trauma response. This response cuts them off from themselves, their surroundings, and other people and can lead to emotional problems and chronic health issues.

So even if what happened was relatively "minor" compared to such egregious crimes as fathers raping their daughters, if the child's nervous system was overwhelmed and they froze—or learned to "fawn" as a way to stay safe by appeasing their abuser—there are ramifications.

It is important to note that if a child could fight off an abuser or run to safety, they would have kept their power, avoided the abuse, and completed the stress response, so they would not have unresolved trauma trapped in their body. I know it felt good when a much older teenager tried to manipulate me into sex acts when I was 13 and I sent him packing with a roundhouse punch to the side of the head. No unresolved trauma there! I did not let him take my power. (And yet I was triggered into the freeze response when my clients harassed me on the job in my 20s. This was because of the power imbalance: if I retaliated, I could lose my job).

As it is, most children are not able to keep their power and may even take on blame that's not theirs. It's so painful they bury the whole mess deep inside but then act out this subconscious material over the course of their lives.

As they grow up, children who were sexually abused often act out their earlier trauma with sexually precocious behaviour—leading to more chances of victimization and more feelings of shame. As adults, they may numb their feelings with alcohol or other substances or harmful habits like overspending or taking risks with their safety. They may find themselves unable to say no in unwanted sexual situations, as they are easily triggered back into freeze.

The shame, lack of boundaries, and easily-triggered nervous system play out in many harmful, self-sabotaging ways, especially for women, who are socialized to put themselves last. Women who were abused as girls are more likely to attract and be attracted to an equally traumatized partner. Mutual dysregulation and lack of boundaries lead to toxic relationship dynamics, and they may stay in these relationships for a long time. They may also stay too long in a soul sucking job, underperform at work, or undercharge their clients. They may struggle to express their needs in relationships and feel a pathological need to fix, save, and over-serve others at their own expense.

But it doesn't have to stay this way.

The first step of the healing journey is to decide that you want to heal and commit to doing whatever it takes. And then you must learn *how* to heal, because knowledge is power. Learning how to heal involves understanding what is actually going on with you, which is why I have explained the mechanisms of childhood trauma as much as space in this chapter allows.

Of course, I did not know any of this for most of my life. I did not understand my anxiety, rage, and shame, my perfectionism and overdoing, my tendency to take risks and get badly injured, my inability to speak my truth, or my desire for self-annihilation. It was only as life served up more and more trauma and I was left shattered at 50 in the aftershock of my divorce that I made it my mission to learn how to heal.

I already had a solid foundation in my long-time yoga practice and the intensive Iyengar yoga teacher training I had done in the 1990s. In my search for more I discovered Reiki, Integrated Energy Therapy, Emotional Freedom Techniques (EFT tapping), and Soul Realignment and became a certified practitioner in all these healing modalities. I devoured everything I could about healing and pursued additional knowledge and training in qigong, acupressure, Feldenkrais, breathwork, Somatic Experiencing, and other body-mind healing techniques. I applied what I learned with myself and my clients with great success and, most of all, I learned to take responsibility for my own thoughts, choices, and feelings and to stand increasingly in my truth and power.

Based on my experience, here is my roadmap for the healing journey:

If you were abused at a young age, make it a priority to reconnect with your inner child. This is of vital importance. SHE NEEDS YOU. This is a visualization and feeling process. Imagine little you after an incident of abuse and go to her, as your adult self, and ask her what she needs.

She may need a hug or words of reassurance, or she may need you to imagine rescuing her and kicking the shit out of her abuser. Your brain registers your visualizations just as if they were real. Feel her relief in your bones.

Allow yourself to grieve for the loss of your childhood innocence and the downstream effects the abuse has had on your life.

Have compassion for yourself in all your struggles and forgive yourself for all your mistakes. You were doing your best at the time with the resources you had.

Pay close attention to your self-talk and interrupt your inner critic every time she starts to slag you. Cancel her and replace her with your ideal nurturing mother-self who offers constructive and supportive words.

Take real care of yourself. Feed yourself well, get lots of fresh air, sunshine, and exercise, take breaks throughout the day, go to bed early, minimize your consumption of alcohol and other substances (which can be calming in the short term but cause problems in the long run), and be careful of consuming negative media laden with violence and fear. You don't need it. You also don't need toxic relationships, so assess your relationships and minimize contact with people who drain or belittle you.

Handwrite your most negative, painful thoughts and feelings and then throw them away—every day, if necessary. Shredding or burning the paper is particularly satisfying. You'll be amazed how good this feels.

Seek and nurture supportive friendships and resist the urge to isolate. We are social creatures, and connecting with others helps us regulate our nervous systems through a process called "co-regulation." Connecting with animals, tending to plants, and spending time in nature are also powerful ways to bring your nervous system to a healthier state.

Practice this powerful exercise: Stand or sit tall and lift your chest, tune into your breath, feel your feet grounding into the Earth, and look around your environment very, very slowly with a soft gaze and relaxed jaw. All of these actions help to unwind the patterns of trauma, which separate us from ourselves and the environment and often leave us shrinking in our bodies, holding our breath, clenching our jaws, and darting our eyes as we desperately seek an escape.

Do physical things like rocking back and forth and hugging and patting yourself. These actions take your body, mind, and nervous system back to your childhood and how you soothed yourself, or the way that others soothed you (or not, making it even more important to soothe yourself now).

Understand that unresolved trauma resides in your body as trapped survival energy (fight, flight, freeze, and fawn) that keeps you stuck in reactive and exhausting survival mode. It does not resolve on its own over time; it just stays there, keeping you anxious, stuck, and struggling to move forward in life. Talk therapy does not resolve trauma—in fact, it can re-traumatize you, because your brain registers your words as if they were happening in real time.

Instead, seek to release trauma through your body and nervous system. Yoga, EFT, breathwork, qigong, Reiki, and somatic exercises are some very effective methods I teach in my programs specifically adapted for healing shame, fear, boundary issues, disempowering social conditioning, negative subconscious programming, and limiting beliefs. Be aware that if you have been severely traumatized, you should seek professional help.

Finally, seek to expand into true self-love, self-nurturance, and self-trust. Make time and space in your life to quiet your mind and learn to be the neutral, all-loving observer of your own thoughts, feelings, and actions rather than identifying with and reacting to everything you think, feel, and do. Remember that you are a soul in a body on a journey and that your Higher Self is always there, waiting for you to drop the distractions and tune in to your divine guidance and true spiritual essence.

You do not need to live your life caught up in the shackles of shame, fear, guilt, anger, and grief, easily triggered into losing your centre and therefore yourself. You can process your emotions, release trauma, take back your power, and make a stand for yourself. From there, you can tap into your natural gifts and your inner resources of intuition, wisdom, love, freedom, satisfaction, and joy. It is such a worthwhile journey.

Monica Linson

Reclaiming Yourself Now

https://www.linkedin.com/in/monica-linson-912693189/
https://www.facebook.com/Reclaiming.Yourself.Now/
https://www.instagram.com/@Reclaiming.Yourself.Now
https://www.reclaimingyourselfnow.com/

Monica Linson is a teacher, abuse recovery coach, and writer. She is dedicated to supporting survivors of narcissistic abuse to reclaim themselves and create a path to a fabulous new life—one that is narcissist-free. Monica knows from personal experience that healing from the abuse will require deep self-awareness and becoming grounded in self-love, confidence and trust.

Having been raised by a covert narcissist, which left her primed to marry one, Monica knows how toxic such relationships can be. Not only are the covert narcissist's tactics subtle, most people see him as Mr. Nice Guy, causing the victim to question herself, and her sanity. That's why Monica's mantra is, "I don't want another woman to do 30-years."

If you find yourself needing to bounce back from a toxic relationship, reach out. Monica will help you to reclaim yourself.

STUCK AT FIVE YEARS OLD

By Monica Linson

Dear Little Me,

I want you to know that I see you and that I love every ounce of you. I love you from your head to your toes. I love your little sweaty nose! (By the way, our nose is still the first place that sweats on hot days or long hikes.) I love you for your vigilance to keep us safe. You did a fabulous job. I know that I wouldn't be here today without your tenacity. Thank you.

Most of all, Little Monica, I want to acknowledge what happened to you with the babysitter's son. Something our Daddy should have done five decades ago. The terror that you experienced is the story of too many little girls. It's a blight that should not be! I admire you, babygirl, for withstanding the weight of the shame and abandonment that you felt when Daddy didn't believe your words and left you vulnerable to more abuse by sending you back. The betrayal that you felt when, for months after, he refused to make eye contact stayed trapped in our body for years. Thank you for figuring out early on that the best way to reclaim his attention, love, and affection was to prove yourself useful. Useful you proved to be. Still, Daddy had his own demons and was incapable of loving you the way we needed to be loved. Make no mistake, your efforts paid off! You secured a place in his heart, and he remembered us until the very end, long after many other memories had fallen away,

I want you to know, Little Me, that what happened to you at Norma's house was not your fault. I know that you've heard those words before from therapists along the way, but I want you to hear them from me. What happened to you is not your fault. No one has a right to touch you there, or anywhere on your body, without your permission. NO! Means no; STOP! Means stop. Both are complete sentences that are easily understood. It wasn't your fault that your words were ignored. Ray... Eric... Venetia...

*Calvin… Huck… and John. They all knew better! They chose **wrong**. That's theirs to own. Not yours. Not ours.*

I know that you blamed yourself for what happened. Trust me when I tell you that the scriptures Hebrew 13:4 and Ephesians 5:3 did not apply to you. No matter what Daddy said. You were not guilty of fornication. You did not act immorally. You were a child, just 5-years old, the first time it happened.

I'm here to tell you that I understand why you came to see the world as a dangerous place. For you, it was! But I'm here now. I've been able to make sense of the chaos—some of it, anyway. I'm here to keep us safe. I'm following your example and speaking up, telling our truth loud and clear until someone hears me. I've got this. You no longer have to stand guard. You can play, take a nap, or enjoy a game of Jacks. You've done enough.

~~*

Above is part of a letter I wrote to my younger self to validate her experience and honor the pain that she endured. It wasn't until I healed the wounds of Little Me that I could say, "Me too, but never again!" What happened to me between the ages of five and fourteen determined the lens through which I navigated life. Looking back, I can see how the trauma of childhood sexual abuse oozed into the nooks and crannies of my being. The shame that I felt about what happened to me stifled my courage, stole my dreams, and set me up to mistake familiarity for love.

Worst of all, it allowed me to stay in a toxic marriage for far too long. When I met the man I was to marry, he was funny, charming, thoughtful, and kind. He made promises that my heart longed to hear. He appeared to be safe. When the mask fell away, and the invalidation, cruelty, and betrayals surfaced, the five-year-old version of me knew exactly what to do. I adjusted my expectations and way of being to accept the love he thought I was worthy of instead of the love I truly deserved.

The shift to prioritizing the wants and needs of my then-husband over my own was swift, smooth, and natural. Not because I was in a marriage filled with respect and reciprocity but because it was the strategy Little Me had devised decades before in order to get whatever love and attention she could from our father and to keep us as safe as possible. Throughout my twenties, thirties, and forties, I used the same strategy. Subconsciously, I tried to erase the shame of sexual abuse and prove that I was worthy of love by accommodating the needs of others. It didn't matter if the needs were physical, mental, emotional, or financial. Everyone else's wishes came before my own. Doing and giving became my default settings.

It wasn't until after the implosion of my thirty-year marriage to a covert narcissist that I was able to see all the red flags that had been there since the beginning. He had been diagnosed with narcissistic personality disorder years before. Yet, I stayed. I stayed, despite the apathy, lies, and entitlement. Following a great deal of soul searching and tears, as I asked and answered some very tough questions, I realized that my need to be loved, seen, and heard, and worthy of my father's protection was so great that I dismissed the warning signs. The wound of my five-year-old self was still open and needed care. My Little Me yearned to know that she didn't need to earn the right to become someone that didn't deserve to be sexually violated. She already was that person. We all are. My Little Me needed to know that the perversions and cruelty of others do not reflect her value. On the contrary, it reflects the brokenness and cowardice of the perpetrators.

Now that I have healed the wounding of my five-year old self, and as I keep a protective eye on my 8, 11, and 14 year-old selves, I have become my greatest source of love and devotion. Loving someone in hopes that they will love me back is no longer my default setting. My own needs are my highest priority. No more invalidating myself for someone else's comfort. I keep myself safe by honoring and trusting myself.

I invite you to heal your wounds from childhood sexual trauma. Become aware of the beliefs that *little you* came up with to make sense of the chaos, beliefs that still influence your life today. Allow your younger self, the one who got you through the tough times, to be seen and heard. Validate her experience. Honor her pain. Look her in the eyes and tell her that she is loved and appreciated. It will take courage and resilience. But you've got those. I know, because you're still here.

JOIN THE MOVEMENT!
#BAUW

Becoming An Unstoppable Woman
With She Rises Studios

She Rises Studios was founded by Hanna Olivas and Adriana Luna Carlos, the mother-daughter duo, in mid-2020 as they saw a need to help empower women around the world. They are the podcast hosts of the *She Rises Studios Podcast* as well as Amazon best-selling authors and motivational speakers who travel the world. Hanna and Adriana are the movement creators of #BAUW - Becoming An Unstoppable Woman: The movement has been created to universally impact women of all ages, at whatever stage of life, to overcome insecurities, and adversities, and develop an unstoppable mindset. She Rises Studios educates, celebrates, and empowers women globally.

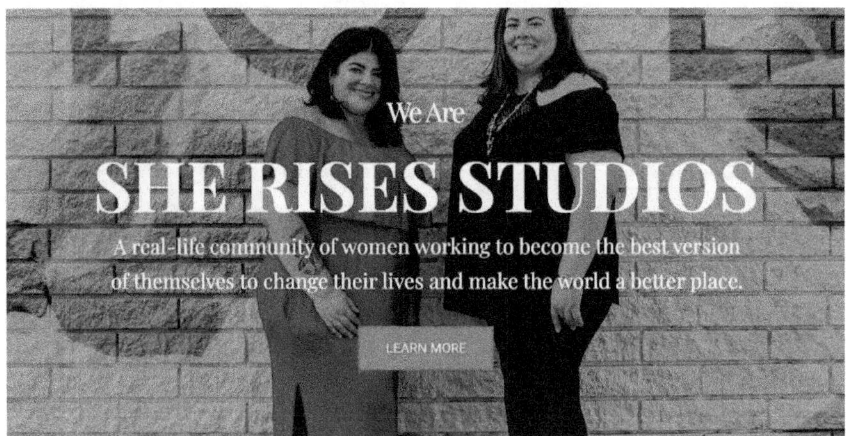

Looking to Join Us in our Next Anthology or Publish YOUR Own?

She Rises Studios Publishing offers full-service publishing, marketing, book tour, and campaign services. For more information, contact info@sherisesstudios.com

We are always looking for women who want to share their stories and expertise and feature their businesses on our podcasts, in our books, and in our magazines.

SEE WHAT WE DO

OUR PODCAST

OUR BOOKS

OUR SERVICES

Be featured in the Becoming An Unstoppable Woman magazine, published in 13 countries and sold in all major retailers. Get the visibility you need to LEVEL UP in your business!

Have your own TV show streamed across major platforms like Roku TV, Amazon Fire Stick, Apple TV and more!

Learn to leverage your expertise. Build your online presence and grow your audience with Fenix TV.
https://fenixtv.sherisesstudios.com/

Visit www.SheRisesStudios.com to see how YOU can join the #BAUW movement and help your community to achieve the UNSTOPPABLE mindset.

Have you checked out the *She Rises Studios Podcast?*

Find us on all MAJOR platforms: Spotify, IHeartRadio, Apple Podcasts, Google Podcasts, etc.

Looking to become a sponsor or build a partnership?

Email us at info@sherisesstudios.com